In Praise of the Bicycle

In Praise
of the Bicycle

Marc Augé

Translated by Teresa Lavender Fagan

REAKTION BOOKS

Published by Reaktion Books Ltd
Unit 32, Waterside
44–48 Wharf Road
London N1 7UX, UK

www.reaktionbooks.co.uk

This book was originally published in French as
Éloge de la bicyclette, © 2008, 2010, Editions Payot & Rivages

First published in English 2019
English-language translation © Reaktion Books
English translation by Teresa Lavender Fagan
Illustrations by Philip Waechter

Printed and bound in Malta
by Gutenberg Press Ltd

A catalogue record for this book is available from the British Library

ISBN 978 1 78914 138 2

CONTENTS

The bicycle: from myth to utopia *7*

The Myth Experienced

The myth and history *13*

The discovery of oneself *28*

The discovery of others *35*

The Crisis

The myth in ruins *44*

The urbanization of the world:
in search of the lost city *53*

Escaping the crisis? *57*

Utopia

Bicycle freedom *69*

The youth of the world *77*

The pedal stroke effect *84*

Back on Earth *88*

The bicycle: from myth to utopia

It is impossible to sing the praises of the bicycle without talking about yourself. Bikes are a part of all of our pasts. Learning how to ride a bicycle is a uniquely memorable moment in our childhood or adolescence. When we first began to ride, we discovered what our bodies could do, our physical abilities, and we revelled in the freedom cycling provided. For someone of my generation, talking about the bicycle inevitably brings back memories. But such memories are not just personal, they are rooted in a time and a place, in a history that is shared with millions of others. After the Second World War, the sport of cycling, already hugely popular, assumed epic proportions, especially when the Tour de France was held again in 1947. Cycling events are still largely epic, in spite of the crises they have endured arising from doping scandals and problems in professional sports in general. The current Tour de France crisis is serious for many reasons, mainly because it affects the intimate memory and personal mythology of every French person. But for that very reason the crisis may be resolved: myths are resilient. And what's more, urban planning policies are coming to the rescue. Just when the urbanization of the world has forced anyone wishing to pursue bucolic dreams to seek refuge in tamed, constructed nature (regional parks) or artificial, imagined nature (amusement parks), the miracle of cycling turns cities into lands of adventure or, at the very least, of journeys.

That miracle has for a long time been what makes cities like Amsterdam or Copenhagen so charming. But now, planners in other cities are also beginning to believe in miracles and are attempting, not without difficulty or mistakes, to make it happen, for example in the two French cities that are the most congested with automobile traffic: Paris and Lyon. There are plans to make bicycles readily available to residents and visitors, to bring people back onto the streets, thereby encouraging them to meet and get to know each other, to breathe life into city spaces, create an urban dreamscape. It's not '68 anymore. Today, to change the way we live means we must first change the city. There is much to be done, and what has already been done has not always been done well. But the fact that a utopia has found a home is already something.

The Myth Experienced

The myth and history

Let us begin with a few dates and references. I will cite them all together, in order to describe to those who weren't there something about what it was like during a very specific moment in Europe at the end of the 1940s. Emerging from the worst atrocities in history, in the aftermath of the first atomic bombings, and just before what would soon be called the balance of terror, in a Europe that in many respects had not fully emerged from the nineteenth century, the need to truly live was being expressed like never before. There was a strong working class, and in spite of what some knew or should have known about the ambiguities and crimes of the Soviet camps, workers believed in the future of socialism. The bicycle, an indispensable object for those of lesser means, but also a symbol of dreams and escape, expressed the ambivalence of a situation in which the harshness of everyday life was still measured against promises of the future. Vittorio De Sica's *Bicycle Thieves* was made in 1948, Jacques Tati's *Jour de fête* in 1949. Also in 1949, Fausto Coppi, world cycling champion, won both the Giro d'Italia and the Tour de France. *Bicycle Thieves*, an early master-piece of Italian neorealism, is the story of the ordeals and wanderings of an unemployed man from the outskirts of Rome. He finds a job putting up posters, for which he needs a bicycle, an indispensable mode of transportation, to go from place to place, but he has already pawned his in order to make ends meet. His wife takes her prized dowry linen to the pawn shop to get the bike back. The film portrays a day during which the unfortunate hero has his bicycle stolen, tries to find the thief, and then, kicked out of the neighbourhood where the thief lives, tries to steal a bicycle himself; he is caught and ends the day in shame and despair.

Jour de fête is a burlesque film set in the French countryside. The village postman, played by Tati, is not at all tragic. Gangly, awkward, good-naturedly teased by those around him, he is essentially an imitator. Playing at being a postman the way Sartre's waiter plays at being a waiter, acting like a bicycle racer when he sees a local race fly by in which the young men of the region compete, he exists only to be looked at by others, but no one really looks at him. He incarnates a certain form of solitude and poverty but is portrayed in a light and humorous way.

When he was young, Fausto Coppi worked in a butcher's shop and made deliveries on his bike, as a bit later the baker's son, the future French champion Louison Bobet, would deliver bread and croissants from his family bakery. Achieving his dream of becoming a bicycle racer, Coppi began as a *gregario*, or domestique, for Gino Bartali before becoming the 'perfect hero' Roland Barthes would write about, the champion generations would dream about because he incarnated courage, intelligence, style and misfortune. In a few years he went from the trivialities of neorealism to the splendours of myth. It was a political myth, too, because compared to the conservative Bartali, the idol of the Christian Democrats, Coppi was a son of the people, beloved by the leftist press and, moreover, as a result of an adulterous romantic adventure, earned the ire of the Vatican.

In the same period, all of France was laughing listening to André Bourvil sing 'À bicyclette' (1947), a somewhat naughty song, fairly inane and in the 'Gaulois' tradition of rural comedy, but in which were found, in the mode of parody and comedy, all the 'mythemes' of the cycling legend, the bicycle, the racer and the Tour:

> . . . *Soudain, qui vois-je devant moi?*
> *Un' belle fille au frais minois*
> *À bicyclette.*
> . . .
> *'Est-c'que vous êtes coureur?'*
> *'Non je n'suis pas coureur . . .'*
> . . .
> *'Vous avez fait le Tour?*
> *Tour de France'*
> *'Non, mais j'ai fait des tours . . .'*

. . . Suddenly, who do I see before me?
A lovely fresh-faced girl
On her bicycle.
. . .
'Are you a racer?'
'No, I'm not a racer . . .'
. . .
'Have you ridden the Tour?
the Tour de France'
'No, but I've been around . . . .'

For a myth to be sustained, it must be carried by history; people must be able to recognize in it a transcendent form of what they are living. And so it is not surprising that the bicycle and champion cyclists were objects of a sort of popular cult before the war, in an era of paid holidays during which, in 1936, 1937 and 1938, bicycles and tandems invaded French roads, as well as in the post-war years, when many workers continued to ride their bikes to their jobs.

If the cult in France today appears to be faltering more rapidly than in other European countries,

it is probably because the link between everyday life and the myth has been greatly relaxed, if not broken. The greater distances between where people live and where they work, and the systematic use of cars, have relegated the bicycle to the realm of sports or leisure. 'Bikers' teem on the roads on Sunday; a few young people still dream of a career in racing, but French champions are rare. Track racing, which already fascinated Toulouse-Lautrec at the end of the nineteenth century, when the writer Tristan Bernard was athletic director of the Vélodrome Buffalo (I'm thinking of Toulouse-Lautrec's drawing *Zimmerman et sa machine*), is a sport that had many followers before the war (it was in the Vel' d'Hiv, the Vélodrome d'Hiver, an indoor cycling track in Paris, that Arletty, Michel Simon and Fernandel met up in *Fric-frac*, the 1939 film by Claude Autant-Lara and Maurice Lehmann) and in the early post-war years, seen notably in the popularization of six-day races, but is no longer a popular form of entertainment in our society, which, however, loves to be entertained. The '*petite reine*' (the 'little queen', an 1891 French expression highlighting the reign of the bicycle) is not what it used to be. Races such as the Paris–Roubaix – the 'Hell of the North' – have lost their auras at the same time that industry is withering away in northern France. The Bordeaux–Paris race disappeared in 1988. Regional races such as the Tour de l'Ouest have been gone for quite some time, whereas back in the day the most prestigious racers competed eagerly – and brilliantly – in them. In France, at least, we are no longer much interested in the great classic races, such as the Liège–Bastogne–Liège, Milan–San Remo or the Giro di Lombardia. Though the Tour de France still attracts crowds, other races in the country of Bobet, Jacques Anquetil and Bernard Hinault are much less prestigious than they were just a few decades ago. However, in Scandinavian countries, Italy and Spain, where the bicycle has maintained a more popular, daily, functional use (associated with professional activities) than in France, there is more interest in small, regional races. In France, it is because the myth is fading that the French no longer win races, and not the reverse. There is still the Tour de France, however, which occupied such a place in the French imaginary up until the 1980s that even thirty-somethings today would be traumatized should the threats that weigh on it come to pass and it disappear, taking with it a part of their personal mythology. Since myth also involves words, we can be sure that it is still being conveyed from generation to generation along the roads of the Tour, and that it will take some time for that myth to be erased from the collective memory, even if the race is no longer held. The Tour de France, with its illusions, is a 'space of memory' par excellence.

After the war, I was old enough to go to the barber's alone ('parted on the left side and shaved close around the ears,' I would recite scrupulously), and I indulged in a forbidden pleasure: reading the sports magazines *But* (Goal) and *Miroir Sprint*, the latter of which was launched in 1946. It was a weekly publication that leaned to the Left and the Communist Party. *But et Club* was created in 1947 by Gaston Bénac with the help of Félix Lévitan, a sports reporter who in 1962 became director of the daily newspaper *Le Parisien libéré* and co-organizer of the Tour de France. In the same year, *But et Club* acquired *Le Miroir des sports*, which had been banned from publication in 1944 because it had appeared under the Occupation. *Le Miroir des sports* was at first the subtitle of *But et Club*, but in 1956 simply replaced it. The stated goal of this move was to counter the influence of *Miroir Sprint*, but both weeklies would disappear after 1968, when their audience's hunger for images began to be sated by television. I was oblivious to all these historical and political considerations when, around 1950, in the barber's shop, I plunged my nose into those magazines filled with photos of the faces of six-day racers, or of my legendary heroes, from Jean Robic to Coppi.

In Brittany, where I spent my summer holidays, bikes were popular to say the least. Fishermen would go to the ports in the area on their bikes, and every morning and evening their wives would do the same, riding to and from their jobs at the jam factory, even when it rained or was very windy. The round-trips of these folks punctuated their days. My itineraries on the blue bike that my grandfather had given me were less serious, but during the month of July I would find myself around four or five o'clock every evening in front of the café on the place de l'Église. The owner would hang a blackboard next to the door on which he had written the names of the first-, second- and third-place winners of the day's stage of the Tour, and the first three names in the general classification. That is where, in 1949 and 1952, my admiration for Coppi, and my elation when his victory was announced, definitively rid me of any national chauvinism. I never felt the same overwhelming admiration for a French champion – and notably not for Bobet (who won the Tour in 1953) – as I had for Coppi.

When you think about the Tour de France, the *Iliad* and the *Odyssey* might come to mind; perhaps the *Iliad* more than the *Odyssey*, because it is the daily battles of the heroes that capture your attention. I experienced that epic without thinking about it, and it naturally found sustenance and a vocabulary in the newspapers I read feverishly every morning – or rather, more specifically, *Le Télégramme*, the only newspaper other than *Ouest-France* to reach my grandparents' village. I despised the 'wheel-suckers'. I was always afraid that, like Rik Van Steenbergen, the king of the sprinters, they would snatch world championship victory from my favourite. I admired Fiorenzo Magni, with his bald head and huge forehead, the king of descents, but preferred the climbers. I believed in the 'Justices of the Peace' (the steepest cols in the Alps) the way one believes in justice. The jokes of Abdel-Kader Zaaf, the lanterne rouge or red lantern, were hilarious.

In *Mythologies* (1957), Roland Barthes magnif-
icently analyses the rhetorical phrases used by the
printed press and radio presenters in which they
naturalized the men and humanized nature in their
reporting, thereby contributing to their epic character. But his analysis is strictly semiological and
was contemporary to the event. He was about forty
years old in 1955, around which time he became
interested in the portraits the press and the radio
painted of the heroes of the moment. That moment
was that of the great French team (with the Bobet
brothers, the Lazaridès brothers, Raphaël Geminiani
and Antonin Rolland, faithful grouches, and also
André Darrigade, the 'Greyhound of the Landes',
almost always unbeatable in the final sprint). It was
a moment that came soon after – but after nevertheless – one that was unforgettably emotional for me,
because the reign of Bobet came immediately after
that of Coppi. In his analysis Barthes doesn't deal
with the Tour over time, and doesn't tell us (that
isn't his intent) if he remembers the Tours de France
from before the war, the Tours de France of his

childhood. However, we can assess the passing of time by reading him again today, because the mythology of the Tour is no longer the one he deconstructs with such finesse, even if, like a ghost, it still haunts the imaginations of many of those who continue to watch the racers in the *Grande Boucle* – the Great Tour Loop – fly by while encouraging them with gestures and shouts.

Remaining for a moment with the Tour de France, which is probably the best-known cycling event in the world, it seems to me that its organizers have missed the boat in Europe; rather, they have created a commercial image of it which, we may fear, corresponds to certain aspects of reality. It is indeed paradoxical that at a time when everyone is talking about Europe, the sport of cycling is no longer the popular bulwark of regional, national and European geography. The substitution of corporate teams for national or regional teams (let us recall that, in the 1950s, French cycling was so rich that it could support several regional Tour teams) has ultimately sanctioned the triumph of the consumer society. The

Tour de France has gone directly from its national dimension to commercial globalization by short-circuiting the European dimension. Regional and national teams disappeared in 1961, despite their ephemeral resurgence in 1967 and 1968. To highlight the European dimension of the Tour de France, on sixteen occasions since 1947 it has started in a different country close to France.

The first start city outside France was Amsterdam in 1954. But there have never been any European teams (alongside which national teams would have played the role of the former regional teams) that might have challenged teams from North or South America, Asia or Australia. It is a fact that attempts to create a cycling Tour of Europe have been abandoned, as if the sport of cycling, true to its popular roots, had remained revelatory of political problems. Thus the cycling myth is doubly detached from its political dimension: the bicycle no longer has the same role in the popular segments of society, and the sport of cycling, despite the amazing and intelligent contributions of television, contributes less and less to feeding the geographical, national and political imaginary. Can a sport without a space still find its place?

The discovery of oneself

The myth is all the stronger if it resonates with those to whom it is told. In Brittany in the 1950s, every teenager tried to sprint, to show off by letting go of the handlebars on the flats and on descents, or by dancing on the pedals to get up the steepest hills – in short, to act as if their ordinary bikes were the most spectacular racing machines. Somewhat like the postman in *Jour de fête*, but taking themselves a bit more seriously – more like the tall teenaged boy who, in Jacques Tati's *Monsieur Hulot's Holiday*, struts with great swagger under the balcony of a young Parisian girl on holiday. In 1953 Tati provided a wonderful, healthy, humorous lesson for the male teenagers of the time. There was the same humour and tenderness fifteen years later in the 1968 song 'À bicyclette' by Pierre Barouh and Francis Lai, sung by Yves Montand. At that time, several generations recognized themselves in the song because in it they rediscovered either real or dreamed memories of their adolescence:

> *Quand on partait de bon matin*
> *Quand on partait sur les chemins*
> *À bicyclette . . .*

> When we left early in the morning
> When we set off on the roads
> On our bicycles . . .

But the humour and tenderness wouldn't have exercised such powerful charm if riding a bicycle for teenagers in the 1930s, '40s or '50s hadn't first represented an extraordinary newfound freedom.

When you start pedalling, you acquire a new form of autonomy; it's an escape, a tangible freedom, movement powered from the bottom of your foot, when the machine responds to the body's desire to move and almost anticipates it. In a few seconds, the limited horizon is expanded, the landscape moves. You are somewhere else. You become someone else, and yet you are yourself as never before; you are what you are discovering.

When I think back on my first cycling adventures I am well aware that they were very tame and very modest. But that didn't matter. From the day I achieved bicycling autonomy, my world was wonderfully enlarged. In Brittany, the few square kilometres that were opened up to me in turn opened up new worlds: the sea on one side (beaches along little roads, the fishing boat port by the main highway), the countryside and the forest on the other (the adventure of hunting mushrooms starting at the end of August). This physical connection with space was a novel and exalting experience of solitude. The physical connection with myself was an intimate experience: I was learning about my abilities and my limits – you can't cheat when you're riding a bike. Any excessive presumption of strength is immediately punished. My bike had only three speeds, but I had to learn how to use all three gears if I didn't want to have to stop on the steep hill I bravely climbed on my way home and if I wanted to avoid the shame of entering the village pushing my bike. I learned how to shift gears, I was disciplined, and when at the end of the holiday I was able to climb up to the place de l'Église in third gear without dancing on the pedals, I knew I had become stronger.

We know that, just like the skill of swimming, which stays with you forever, you never forget how to ride a bike. But there is more to it than that. The progressive learning about yourself that is intimately connected to learning how to ride a bike leaves traces that are unconscious yet unforgettable. This is a paradox that makes the process unique. It is a paradox of time and eternity, if you like. Youngsters who begin to ride a bike experience a mastery of their bodies. It is an experience of mastery because they are, as has been said, in the prime of life. More or less resilient, more or less fast, more or less talented, but in principle all vigorous, they measure themselves against the challenges of the terrain by throwing themselves into it. They know they are stronger at certain moments than at others. In their

strongest moments they experience the sensation of *en avoir sous la pédale* – 'having it under the pedal', having a burst of strength – as a colourful popular French expression puts it. This sensation fades with exertion and disappears in a few hours, giving way to fatigue. It becomes increasingly rare as you age, especially if you don't train. In this respect, to ride a bike is to learn how to manage time, both the short time of the riding day or of a racing stage and the long time of the years that add up. And yet (and this is another paradox) to ride a bicycle is also to experience eternity. It is a bit like when, on a beach, you lie down on the sand and close your eyes and experience the feeling of being a child again, or, more exactly, experience ageless feelings that escape the corrosive action of time, just like someone who, somewhat timidly at first, gets on a bike after several years of not riding. He or she not only quickly 'rediscovers sensations', as athletes say to describe the awareness they have of their bodies and its abilities as soon as they start training again, but above all quickly rediscovers with them a host of other sensations (the exaltation of the free-wheel descent, the sound of asphalt under the tyres, the air caressing his or her face, the slow movement of the passing landscape) that seemed only to be waiting for that occasion to be reborn.

The discovery of others

Under the ostensible pretext of staying in shape, many older people ride bikes, not every day and not alone, but in groups, on Sundays, sometimes wearing the same jerseys as the professional cyclists today, as if they wanted to support or sing the praises of a European bank, a credit agency or a telephone company. In fact they are playing a game, because their real intent is to rediscover the pleasures of their childhood and engage in childhood activities with their friends. They give each other nicknames and make good-natured fun of each other. They jokingly compare themselves to the champions of the moment, thereby turning themselves into the protégés of those young men through a symbolic ruse whose artificial character becomes apparent with each attempt to accelerate. They consciously pretend they are still young, and by that very fact actually remain fairly 'young'. Thus the bicycle is an important component of the social lives of some seniors in the French provinces. Such biking camaraderie in a person's later years, the camaraderie among retirees, is both sociable and heroic, because it thumbs its nose at old age and death. It is also an occasion for active engagement and contact between generations, because the co-ed 'biking' groups always include a few individuals who are younger than the others and who play the role of discreet mentors while forcing themselves not to display their muscular superiority too overtly in front of their older fellow riders.

The delights of cycling solitude are thus not incompatible with forms of social interaction, and this, I think, is one of the lasting virtues of cycling. Indeed, in the legends of the cycling greats we are moved by gestures of mutual support among heroes, gestures that had nothing to do with team discipline (Coppi and Bartali passing their water bottles back and forth during a terrible stage in the Pyrenees; Coppi, showing great chivalry, letting Bartali win the stage that fell on his 35th birthday). Among cyclists, even at the humblest level, there is an awareness of a certain camaraderie, the awareness of the

challenges and of shared moments, of an intangible something that distinguishes them from everyone else and belongs only to them. This is seen in Paris today in the kindness shown by the men and women who already have some experience in using the urban bike-sharing system Vélib' towards hesitant neophytes who want to start riding. Grouped around the rental terminals, where beginners struggle to understand how to sign up, the more experienced gladly offer explanations and advice. The hierarchy of age is erased or even inverted: in general, the young are the first to jump into a new opportunity, and they feel confident in their technological abilities both with regard to the electronic terminal and to how the bikes work. Granted, the Vélib' bike is a simple machine, but it is somewhat heavy, and you have to learn how to select and remove it, adjust the seat height, and park and return it. Vélib' veterans are quite willing to initiate novices, and this is a novel phenomenon in a city where connections made between strangers are traditionally not very common.

We must therefore credit the bicycle not only with reintroducing the cyclist to his or her own sense of individuality, but with recreating amicable social interactions. Such interactions may be superficial, probably ephemeral, but they always contribute to making our lives a bit happier. There is, moreover, assuredly a connection between the rediscovery of a certain self-awareness and an awareness of the presence of others. This is because cycling, even done sporadically, is an opportunity to experience something like an identity (a certain permanence in time) that allows you to be aware of others (a form of expectation, an openness to the future). Look in the streets at those who have recently been converted to cycling. They talk to each other (about their route, the landscape, the weather) or ride along silently, but are never (or almost never) on their mobile phones. The sight they offer is the exact opposite of the classic scene we witness daily these days on the terrace of any café: that of two people sitting at the same table but having lengthy conversations with invisible interlocutors on their respective mobile phones. The streets, the cafés, the subways and buses today are filled with ghosts that constantly intrude into the lives of those they haunt; they keep them at a distance and prevent them from either looking at the scenery or getting to know their flesh-and-blood neighbours. But for now, those ghosts clearly haven't learned how to ride a bike! Cyclists have opted for direct communication and temporarily reject the tyranny of electronics. 'Let's hope that lasts!' we want to exclaim. May the bicycle become the quiet and efficient means to a rediscovery of social relationships and communication through spoken words and smiles!

The Crisis

C learly, then, the bicycle is mythical, epic, utopian. Of course, you can't be a true devotee
without living for the most part in the present, if
only because of the hazards of riding in traffic, but
the bicycle also appears in tales that simultaneously
take us back to our own personal histories and
involve us in myths that are shared by so many.
Those two pasts are conjoined and make the most
modest of individual memories seem epic. As ever,
a clear awareness of the past can nourish the way
we imagine the future. The bicycle then becomes a
symbol of an ecological future for the city of tomor-
row and of an urban utopia that will save society
from itself. But the myth, the epic and the utopia
require a bit of faith. The test of actual history is a
harsh one; it constantly threatens to relegate those
concepts to the realm of nostalgia, that sad refuge
of those who have become disillusioned with life.
Doesn't the bicycle, a symbol of a vanished working

class, of athletic competitions no longer seen today and of a fantasized urban life, in the harsh reality of a globalized world risk becoming a fantastical instrument of denial, a tool for a society enslaved by the imperatives of consumption – in short, the ultimate illusion?

The myth in ruins

Is the myth dead, and along with it all the epic feats connected to it? Cycling, like professional sports in general, has made progress. Riders today are probably better athletes than their predecessors were (as is the case in other sports, like rugby and tennis, for example). But the spectacle they offer isn't truly comparable to that of their predecessors. Fausto Coppi was able to come from behind with a fifteen-minute deficit over two stages in the Alps. Today, a team of good riders can block the entire field, thwart all attempts to attack, and in the flat stages see to it that an almost identical scenario plays out: there will be a few attacks, one of which might succeed for a time, but then the peloton catches it and there is a massive sprint at the end, resulting in the victory of the fastest. The mountains always play a decisive role in the Tour, but today they are no longer the backdrop for great individual feats of climbing. In the mountain stages the race has become a race of elimination, of wearing down, during which the 'sacrifice' of teammates (whose paid role is to perform that sacrifice) serves to exhaust the other racers who try to overcome them, and it is rare for a racer to climb brilliantly by himself over two consecutive stages. The myth was maintained and invigorated in the past by a true dramatization which could end in only two ways: either the sublime, inspiring victory or the tragic failure of the hero. As in the *Iliad*, it was the most vulnerable heroes, the heroes with an Achilles heel, who were also the most fascinating: Fausto Coppi and Charly Gaul, more so than Louison Bobet or Jacques Anquetil.

In his essay on the Tour de France, Roland Barthes shows how, from the fans' perspective, the riders' state of grace and state of disgrace were closely connected. Let us look at what he says about the *jump* of Charly Gaul, the archangel of irregular performances: if *form* is a natural condition, at once physical, moral and intellectual, *jump* is 'a true electrical impulse that jolts those racers beloved by the gods, allowing them to accomplish superhuman feats'. Gaul 'receives his *jump* through intermittent commerce with the gods; sometimes the gods inhabit him and he is spectacular; sometimes the gods abandon him, his *jump* is extinguished. Charly can do no more.'

We don't talk about *jump* anymore these days, and for good reason: it is too suspicious, as are any signs of weakness that might follow it. The revelations of doping killed off the heroes – they have prevented us from believing in them – and have killed the myth. Barthes saw this very clearly in 1957: 'There is a horrible parody of the *jump* – doping: doping the rider is as criminal, as sacrilegious, as attempting to imitate God; it is stealing from God the privilege of the spark.' But today, there is nothing left to steal from the gods, and no one would dare mention the *jump* of the most recent winners of the Tour de France. Doping itself aims less to bring about blazes of glory, which are immediately suspect, than to ensure the maintenance of *form*. But it is an exceptional form that, each day of the Tour,

enables riders to produce prodigious efforts, though those efforts are not, strictly speaking, spectacular feats of prowess. As a result, when a rider accomplishes something truly extraordinary, suspicions are now raised: there are no longer any mythical heroes. We might say, graciously, that the spectacle of the Tour has become secularized, but it is more accurate to say that it has been pharmaceuticalized. This is what has truly hurt the myth. Of course, it is quite possible that young amateur racers primarily from distressed industrial regions see cycling as a means to pull themselves up economically – this has always been the case with big, popular sports – but (and this is where the problem lies) they might also admit without much reticence that doping has become an inevitable reality.

Doping was already an issue in the 1940s and '50s. Several riders fell victim to it, and Coppi himself admitted to reporters that there was a lot of hypocrisy in the denunciations of certain people. Riders commonly took amphetamines. It was, moreover, a time when drugs were being used just about everywhere, including in intellectual and student milieus, drugs of all sorts – Maxiton, corydrane, Actiphos (amphetamines) – that could be easily obtained from one's family doctor. But doping today is different, and that's why it has such an enormous effect on the image of the heroic and glorious body that accompanies the notion of a champion. To swallow, smoke or be injected with substances, or to change one's blood the way a rider changes jerseys – none of that can take the place of what it means to be a hero in a fan's imagination.

Doping today, from the point of view of a layperson, is more than a way to increase a body's natural abilities; it is a true substitution of substance, something carried out shamefully in the secrecy of backrooms. This is the opposite of what was previously believed, of the notion of a hero, a notion we desperately cling to. Today's heroic notion reflects a tampering that turns a rider into a purely passive being, an object. But there is also the idea of an intrusion into an intimate realm of the person, either at the moment of doping or at the time of controls, with the taking of blood and urine. Such intrusion touches on a rider's very identity – as if today every laudatory athletic record must necessarily be the result of some wrong done to or by his person. To tell the truth, this perversion of athletic heroism was already under way with the appearance of corporate-sponsored teams, which transformed the riders into human sandwich-boards, into mere marketing tools. The systematic practice of doping completed the transformation of riders into passive instruments of marketing strategies. Of course, the companies that employ them reject them as soon as their 'dishonour' has been revealed, and begin to look for other instruments. But they thereby confirm that it is in fact more difficult to create myths with commercial brands than it is through nations or provinces. When a rider no longer races for his country, the flag-waving and openly nationalistic support of his fans is concentrated more on the individual, just when he has become depersonalized through marketing techniques and the initiatives of 'sports medicine'. It is the end of the myth, the death of the epic.

It is perhaps the end of the myth, but we still have a few memories of it (like those images of the Popular Front and of the first paid holidays in France, when many people set off on their bikes or on tandems). And it is perhaps the death of the epic, definitively relegated to the past but survived by a desire nonetheless, a desire for myth and epic, which always come back to life whenever we see a frail-looking figure, captured by TV cameras, attempting to power his way up a mountain. The image, at that moment, resuscitates the legend. With alternating close-ups, which allow the viewer to see in gritty detail every grimace on a struggling face, and panoramic views that reveal the immensity of grandiose landscapes, live televised coverage is able to portray the moment Barthes was talking about. That moment is the fragile moment of History, 'when man, even clumsy and gullible, through his impure fables nevertheless in his own way envisions a perfect adequation between himself, the community and the universe'. And so the myth and the epic are perhaps still kept alive by the desire they arouse – and continue to thwart.

The urbanization of the world:
in search of the lost city

What about utopia? Is the transformation of cities a conceivable dream, and does the bicycle have a role to play in such a revolution? Because it would indeed take a revolution, in the literal sense, to transform cities. But what, in fact, is the city today?

The urbanization of the world is characterized by both a growth of megalopolises and the extension of 'urban filaments', to borrow the expression of the French historian and demographer Hervé Le Bras, along roads, rivers and coastlines. It conveys the fact that the political and economic life of the planet today depends on decision-making centres located in large global cities, all interconnected and together forming a sort of 'virtual meta-city', according to Paul Virilio. The world has become a world/city, inside which circulate and are traded all categories of products, including information, images, art and fashion. But it is also true that every large city is a world, the world in microcosm, with its ethnic, cultural, social and economic diversity. The divisions whose existence we might sometimes forget in the fascinating spectacle of globalization can be found in fissures in the urban fabric. The city/world, through its very existence, disproves the illusions of the world/city. In urban business centres, buildings known the world over for having been conceived by internationally renowned architects, and which symbolize global business communications, are actually inaccessible in the cities where they are located to those who don't work in them. At the intersection of the world/city and the city/world, it sometimes seems that the city itself is disappearing. Granted, urbanization expands from all directions, but changes in the way work is organized, and technologies that, through television and the Internet, bombard individuals with images of an extensive and omnipresent centre, render obsolete any city/countryside or urban/ non-urban dichotomies.

The world/city, city/world opposition is, in a way, the visible, spatial expression of globalization conceived as the planetary ensemble of means of circulation and networks of communication and distribution. In *The Information Bomb* (1998) Paul Virilio points out that this global ensemble was considered by American Pentagon strategists to be the interior of a world in which the local had been relegated to the exterior. But such a reversal has become even more generalized, and today the big city is defined by its ability to turn outward. On the one hand, it hopes to attract foreign tourists. On the other, urbanism is ruled by the need to facilitate access to airports, train stations and large transportation arteries. The ability to easily enter into and depart from a city is the number-one imperative, as if the balance of the city rested on its external counterweights. The city is becoming decentred the way homes are decentred with tele-visions and computers, and the way individuals have been decentred ever since their mobile phones became both computers and televisions. The urban extends everywhere, but we have lost the city, and we are losing sight of ourselves. And so, yes, perhaps the bicycle has a determining role to play in help-ing humans regain an awareness of themselves and of the places where they live. Bicycles, as regards the lives of the people who ride them, might invert the movement that is projecting cities outside themselves. We need the bicycle to recentre our-selves onto ourselves, by recentring ourselves on the places where we live.

What is at stake in resorting to the bicycle is thus not inconsequential. It involves knowing whether, faced with the rise of a teeming urbanism that threat-ens to reduce the former city to an empty shell, we wish to transform the city into a facade for tourists or an open-air museum, or whether the bicycle, with its symbolic dimension and historical ability to en-courage impromptu encounters, can be restored. It is quite simply a matter of giving fate back its pres-tige, of beginning to break down physical, social or mental barriers that are stifling the city, and to give meaning back to the lovely word 'mobility'.

Escaping the crisis?

From this point of view, the Paris Vélib' bike-sharing programme seems in all respects to be a success. First of all, it has the perfect name ('Vélib' is from *vélo* and *liberté*), and with the increasing number of docking stations throughout Paris where it is possible to pick up or return a bike, it really does give its users a great deal of freedom. With a bit of imagination, it might even be possible to envision a city in which every inhabitant could easily take any bicycle left on the street, leave it anywhere, and pick up another one a bit later – to envision a sort of urban communism for bike riders, united by a common ethics and unanimously respected rules of common courtesy. In August 2007 we witnessed something that resembled such a utopia unfolding in ubiquitous pedal strokes in the streets of Paris. The surge of shared bike users has clearly enabled them to take back the urban space. The Paris *flâneurs* – that species that we thought was becoming extinct – had reappeared . . . but on bikes. The new *flâneurs*, their noses in the wind, were evidently making a double discovery: they were realizing with wonder that the city is meant to be looked at, to be seen (seen directly, without the intervention of a still or movie camera), that it is beautiful, even its most modest streets, and that it is easy to travel around. A bicycle, for those who dare to ride in the city for the first time, is an opportunity for a unique experience. It enables the rider to re-evaluate distances and bring places together in a way that public transportation, which follows set itineraries, doesn't allow. On a bicycle, you don't need to change buses or make train connections. You slip surreptitiously into another eminently and literally *poetic* geography. Riding a bicycle is an opportunity to make swift connections between places you usually visit sep-arately. And the experience thus appears to be a source of spatial metaphors, unexpected connec-tions and short-circuits created continuously using the strength of one's own legs, and an experience of awakened curiosity for new riders. In just a few pedal strokes you can go from Montparnasse to the Eiffel Tower, cross the Seine, linger on a bridge to gaze at the Île de la Cité or the foliage of the Tuileries, head north, lose yourself in the narrow streets of a bygone Paris, go back down to the Bastille and the Marais, turn towards the Bois de Vincennes – which isn't far – or go back to Montparnasse to complete the loop. This is the new freedom, the new freedom of inspiration, enabled by riding a bike. The bicycle is a form of writing, an often free, even wild, form of writing – the experience of automatic writing, active surrealism, or, on the contrary, a more constructed, more developed and systematic meditation, almost experimental, through places that had been previously selected through the refined taste of the knowledgeable.

But there is an obvious dual risk in the bike-sharing experiment currently under way in Paris. The first is that it might rapidly become a summer attraction, reserved for the young and for tourists, a means to sell the capital to those who want to visit it. The second risk is that it could lead to confrontations between drivers and cyclists, fed by a lack of knowledge on both sides, a lack of knowledge about cities and a lack of courtesy, seen in the disgust of drivers most opposed to cyclists as well as in the most wilful disregard of some cyclists who are resolutely disrespectful of traffic rules. Already, and this seems to have been prevalent in France for some time, there is talk of policing and repression, which would stop cold any hope of encouraging a combination of common courtesy, positivity, order and relaxation. The two risks are obviously complementary, and it is clear that the Vélib' bike-sharing programme can be a real, complete and incontestable success only when people of all ages begin to consider it natural to pick up a bike at a station closest to them and dock it near their place of work, or wherever they do their shopping, for example. This assumes that people would no longer be afraid of vehicle traffic or accidents, that a number of accommodations for cyclists would be made, that true cycling lanes would exist everywhere, and that the fate of cyclists won't depend on their agility or

on the goodwill and patience of bus or taxi drivers. Regardless of the recognized expertise of Paris bus drivers, you will never convince a slightly inexperienced or older cyclist (those whose use of a bicycle would already be a criterion for Vélib' success) not to be nervous at the idea of being passed by a bus in a narrow street.

Figures have been published by the Sécurité Routière for the City of Paris, and associations such as the MDB (Mieux se Déplacer à Bicyclette – 'get around better on a bike'). There were two cyclists killed in Paris in 2000, five in 2001. In 2000 there were seventeen seriously injured. The figures are more impressive if one looks at the Paris region: 83 seriously injured and 28 killed in 2000. In Paris, the number of bikes has increased since 2001 (48 per cent) without the number of riders killed increasing proportionately; in 2005 there were three killed and 32 seriously injured. There are still safety issues to be dealt with, however, since the number of accidents involving cyclists increased 8 per cent between 2004 and 2005. In the first six months of 2007, three cyclists were killed and there was a clear increase in the number of those seriously injured. In October 2007 a Vélib' user was killed. A British comedian pointed out that in London there were more cycling victims than victims of terrorism, and he was particularly critical of the Lycra-wearing athletes who speed around recklessly on the streets as well as on the pavements of London, greatly endangering pedestrians, who are bumped into and frightened.

Furthermore, though in 2005 the extent of bike lanes in Paris increased to 327 kilometres (34 of which were created in 2005), their locations do indeed seem to favour the peripheral boulevards and green spaces. The fact that the Vélib' programme stops at the *intra-muros* Paris border is significant from this point of view. The city has understood this, moreover, and at the end of 2007 discussions were held with suburban municipalities. The question of the future of the bicycle in Paris (leisure activity or for daily use?) remains open. We cannot therefore claim today that bicycle use has responded to the challenges of the new urban organization. There has not yet been a cycling revolution.

But there are other examples throughout the world that we can observe and study which show that the idea of a city where bicycle traffic would predominate is not purely a fantasy. In addition to northern European cities (Amsterdam, for example) and a few French cities like La Rochelle, I am thinking of various mid-size Italian cities such as Modena, Bologna or Parma, whose quality of life is obvious to any foreign visitor, especially when they see cyclists riding along in every direction, completely relaxed. Paris isn't Modena, but it isn't Los Angeles, either – that is, a place conceived for automobile traffic. It would certainly be more realistic for the administrators of the city of Paris to use Modena rather than Los Angeles as a model. The challenge comes from the difficulty of reconciling the demands of a global megalopolis (the decentring and extraversion of an ensemble open to the world, which every day imports and exports people, goods, images and information), with those of the city conceived as a place to live, an intimate space strong with its own bearings and daily rhythms.

If our world of images, communication and consumption is tending increasingly to stifle any thoughts about the future and to crush them under the realities of the present, perhaps conditions are nonetheless ripe today to conceive of an effective urban utopia – that is, one that's likely to convince those who live in the city. The paradox of this utopia is that we know where it can exist, even if we struggle to define its limits and borders (where does the city of today begin and end?). The fact that bicycle use would enable those limits and boundaries to be redrawn, inventing unexpected itineraries and reconfiguring the real city – that of everyday uses, exchanges and encounters – is the new and surprising potential that is being timidly revealed, thereby giving us a rare chance to imagine the future without fear or loathing. That opportunity is not at all insignificant or trivial, and it fully justifies the plans that are being made to achieve it, to celebrate it, in the near future. There is the hope that, for once, imagining the future may direct the present narrative, cause society to move, displace established lines and eliminate the fear or pessimism of the less imaginative.

Utopia

Bicycle freedom

Let us allow our imaginations to run wild. Let's imagine a city, a large city – Paris, for example – in thirty years' time. The problem of traffic has been resolved once and for all. Abundant tramways, buses and subways now extend to the furthest edges of the former Paris region. Public transportation has made obsolete the traditional configuration of *intra-muros* Paris. In this vast agglomeration, transversal routes, whose numbers increase every day, connect one point of the city to another in the most direct possible way. Between 5 and 9 a.m., delivery vehicles do their work. Of course, emergency vehicles (ambulances, doctors, firemen, police) have priority status. For everyone else, huge parking towers designed by the greatest architects on the planet, built at various locations on the edges of Greater Paris, constitute monumental 'places of interest' which tourists love to visit. Car and motorcycle drivers retrieve their vehicles there when they want to leave the city. Some incorrigibles have preferred to keep their cars as close to them as possible and use expensive garages in their office buildings. They have been granted authorization which enables them to leave Paris or go home by taking one of the four vehicular routes reserved for cars. Authorization isn't granted to new vehicles, and so it is expected that those four reserved routes will eventually disappear. Since virtually all car traffic within the city limits has been banned, the overall expanse for moving around has been greatly extended with the removal of parking spaces. Vehicles with exemptions – trams, buses and taxis – thus move around freely in their own lanes. For everyone else, the streets belong to cyclists, and the pavements to pedestrians.

Bike-sharing docks are found in all the large train stations, of course, but also near almost all metro, tram or bus stations. There are also vast bike-parking facilities. Bike-sharing is now used primarily by visitors (Paris is still the number-one tourist destination on the planet), because many

Parisians now own their favourite means of transportation, which they often demark with a little
personal touch, 'personalizing' it (which car owners
once did with their cars, and which Baudrillard
made fun of).

Personalizing bicycles has become much more
refined and inventive than that which was seen
with cars, which mainly involved the displaying
of a few fetish objects – stuffed animals, images of
St Christopher or trinkets of various kinds. At the
beginning of the twenty-first century, many cyclists
reinvented their bikes by altering their shapes. It
must be said that in itself the bike is a small object,
an incorporated object, and not an inhabited space
like a car. You don't fit it out or accessorize it: you
fiddle with it. On the borderline between fiddling
with and fitting out, there are accessories that enable
you to carry a certain number of things: baskets or
panniers. There are also various lights or reflective
devices for safety. On the border between fitting
out and incorporation, there is clothing that riders
prefer to wear when they ride a bike which also

falls within the realm of safety (helmets, vests with reflective taping, and so on) or simply for its comfort or out of habit. And, as in the previous century, riders always choose their bike, its colour, its style, and it only takes a detail to enable it to be recognized immediately among all the others. Patient and loyal, it is a faithful and important companion to its owner; a rider doesn't want to be separated from it. All things being equal, the connection we have with our bicycle somewhat recalls the one described by Aristophanes in Plato's *Symposium*: the true cyclist exists fully only when the lost half of his original being is restored to him, when he is one with it. The connection between the cyclist and his bicycle is a connection of love and, literally, of gratitude, which time doesn't destroy; rather it is strengthened, if necessary, in the form of memory and nostalgia when life has separated them.

Those who tinker with their bikes push the work of 'personalization' even further. Their ingeniousness has no limits. Some riders have even reinvented the bicycle, lengthening the handlebars,

moving the saddle back, theoretically to improve the
output of physical effort, the economical virtues of
which Ivan Illich had praised a few decades earlier
in *Toward a History of Needs* (1978):

> The bicycle is the perfect transducer to match
> man's metabolic energy to the impedance
> of locomotion. Equipped with this tool,
> man outstrips the efficiency of not only all
> machines but all other animals as well.

Some stretch out on their bikes as if on a recliner. Others dominate the street, perched on their machine with huge wheels like stilts. In fact, the desire to be noticed plays a part in their designs: the more original their machine, the more visible they are. Some have even created websites that celebrate their inventiveness. Those sites are popular. You can see those riders coming from a distance on their extravagant machines. You recognize them, you call them by their name or their nickname when you see them go by (some have raised a flag on their bike, a banner with their colours, which can be seen at a distance). They are part of the new street scene. Combining the functional with the enjoyable, others have added a little cart to their bike and travel around Paris markets (which tourists adore) to sell their merchandise. Traditionalists, they attempt to adopt the lost rhythm of bygone years and play the role that a century earlier the seasonal street vendors played. Despite the accelerated warming of the planet and the climate disruptions that continue to surprise those who are older but which the under-thirty crowd consider natural, despite the globalization of the food market, several of these cycle vendors 'act as if', determined to sell chestnuts only in the winter, cherries in the spring, melons in the summer and mushrooms in the autumn. The exact provenance of this so-called seasonal produce or of those products of the so-called seasons is not entirely clear, but it's nice to encourage those merchants of illusion and nostalgia.

In fact, 'retro' has been solidly in fashion for several years, and you can see 'pedicabs' everywhere, those pedal carts inspired by the ones that travelled around the streets of Paris a century earlier during the war and the German occupation. Relatively powerful and absolutely non-polluting motors help the cyclists when they need it; thus they are able easily to carry up to two adults in their little coloured cabs. These 'pedicabs' are very popular with tourists and the elderly. As for integrated electric motors, almost invisible and perfectly silent, they are extremely helpful to all those whose fragility, age or temporary weakness limits them on slightly steep hills, but who regain their strength when they realize that they appear to be pedalling with ease to those who are watching them. The electric motor is an instrument of perfect equality, the only incontestable form of positive discrimination. Tandems have returned to fashion, a lovely symbol of the necessary complicity of couples, and new linguistic expressions have appeared to celebrate friendship and love, such as 'share the tandem' or 'pedal together'. More complicated minds have reinvented bicycles with three saddles. They already existed in 1936, as seen in documentaries of that time. Those films are being increasingly shown again, as if they had in some respects represented an anticipation of what would happen a century later.

The youth of the world

The renaissance of the bicycle has shaken urban geography. Bike lanes that go along the Seine to the west and the east enable people to easily get to Suresnes, the Îles and Meudon in one direction, to join up with the confluent of the Marne in the other. Everywhere, open-air cafés have acquired a second wind. Sunday accordion players and spontaneous waltzing have again become de rigueur. Here, too, a delightful breath of nostalgia floats in the air, but it is a pleasant nostalgia, in the form of a return. Indeed, we are celebrating, or believe we are celebrating, something that resembles a reunion. Children are taught at a very young age how to ride a bike and are encouraged to use it to go to school. With a concern for training and safety, processions are organized every morning and every afternoon for the youngest children, who are thereby initiated into the discipline of riding in a group. They follow indicated routes and pass by fixed points that are also meeting spots where parents can come to pick up their children from just a short bike ride away. Together, girls and boys learn about their bodies and about mobility. All schools are involved. It has been some time since religious fundamentalism has had to cede before the bike, and the generalized use of bicycles has definitively freed the few girls whose parents or retrograde brothers were holding them back or were attempting to prevent them from straddling the satanic machine. We are reminded that very early on, at the outset, at the end of the nineteenth century in the United States and Europe, the bicycle had been an instrument for the liberation of women, who, with their puffy trousers or bloomers, had dared to confront the prudish, old-fashioned mores of all types of sexists. History is slow, but it does advance, stress the more optimistic. And now, today, youth from working-class neighbourhoods are mixing on the streets of Île-de-France with those from more affluent areas, all genders included. A new network of youth hostels has been established, and young people again discover landscapes without resorting to television. It is 1936 once again, but without the looming threat of war on the horizon.

PEOPLE ARE BREATHING more easily. Once again, the scents of the chestnut trees in the spring and of grilled chestnuts in the winter have become noticeable, just as are the various odours we had stopped smelling without even realizing it. We rediscover the scents of flowers, fruit, the shellfish and fish laid out on market stalls, that of clean laundry or cologne, and that of the air itself, which has been taking on a little whiff of red wine for some time and which many attempt to breathe in in large gulps to get drunk. The most popular singer is again Charles Trenet: *Y'a d'la joie* ... (There's joy ...)

Also contributing to the pleasantness of the streets is the rediscovered calm of all drivers. Taxi drivers are now always courteous, always in a good mood, always available, and they drive patiently without grumbling. The political situation no longer inspires their acerbic comments. They no longer pile up at airports to avoid city traffic, and you need only

to inadvertently scratch your ear or nose for one to immediately stop in front of you and ask if you require his services. Traffic cops have very little work and are generally in a good mood; police officers are rare and are always pleasant when they appear. It must be said that the cycling industry and all its affiliated services have given a serious nudge to economic growth. The car industry isn't doing too badly and doesn't seem to be suffering too greatly from the freeing of urban space. Pleasure vehicles have increased – small convertibles and little cars of all sorts for holiday travels – and the enormous effort to develop public transportation has led to a true economic boom.

The prestige of the bicycle is such that the sport of cycling has made a comeback, in unexpected forms. Amateur sports have been revived, with cycling competitions between high schools or universities. The University Tour de France is an event that is increasingly followed on television. It's a competition, in a sense semi-professional because there are prizes, but prizes that are made up of training scholarships financed by corporations or public authorities. The stages are short so that the racers aren't overwhelmed; feeding stops are unstructured, and you sometimes see competitors sitting on the edge of the road sharing a snack with spectators before setting off, sticking out their tongues at a peak in the Alps. At the Olympic Games, from which the professional sport has been definitively banned, cycling trials on tracks and on the road are very popular with the fans: contestants are obviously talented young people, but their timed performances are much more modest than those recorded in the last years of 'professionalism'. The stopwatch was reset, as they say, and the record book reopened. Some wanted to push reform further and do away with the notion of records, but they didn't win. National and international meetings were held, and the radicals had to cede before those who pointed out that the notion of records reflected a struggle with oneself, that it was the apex of personal development and not at all a reflection on others. The reform of the sport of cycling unleashed a more general reflection and led to revolutionary changes in all sports. The media supported the movement when they realized the public was behind it and understood the new publicity marketing perspectives that were thus opened to them. Amateur sports replaced reality TV; it is now called 'verity TV', to stress that all fiction is excluded from it, and all broadcasts of sports verity TV are a huge hit.

The pedal stroke effect

The 'pedal stroke effect' is the new fashionable expression. It has replaced the expression 'butterfly effect'. You may recall the lecture given by the meteorologist Edward Lorenz in 1972 and the provocative question he used as a title: 'Does the Flap of a Butterfly's Wings in Brazil Set Off a Tornado in Texas?' Social science researchers today ask themselves whether chaos theory might not be applied even more relevantly to global reality. With the sharp sense of retrospective predictability that often characterizes them, they point out that perhaps everything started one day with a municipal initiative in a city in northern Europe, to essentially and officially protect the first pedal stroke of a city rider. The example stuck, as we've seen in France, first in a few small cities and then in Lyon and Paris, and quickly in all other French cities, but also, and even more so, in all the large metropolises throughout the world. The change in quality of life and the improvement in the ecological health of the planet are obvious benefits for the most part, but the collateral effects are in fact stupefying, notably in the social and political realms. Class barriers have opened or collapsed. Powerful oil companies have fewer and fewer customers, and, facing consequences that delight the more cynical of observers, religious proselytizing has faded away. It seems as if cycling polytheism has overcome petroleum monotheism. Granted, there is fierce competition among bicycle manufacturers for sales, but the potential customer base has become enormous and its demands insatiable. African bikes are challenging bikes made in Asia. We are seeing an increasing number of new and newly rediscovered designs (folding bikes, portable bikes, convertible bikes, bikes with invisible assistance, musical bikes, submersible bikes, aquatic bikes, sail bikes…). Scientists are working on means to capture and transform the energy expended in pedalling; experimental, specially built roads are being constructed for tests. The hope is that entire spans of the energy grid will be fed by the pedalling of cyclists.

Some observers occasionally express the fear that the initial freshness of the global cycling movement will decline over the long term. In the meantime, enthusiasm is intact. To the call of a certain number of governments – 'Cyclists of all countries, unite!' – huge festivals have brought together millions of people of all ages in Beijing, San Francisco and Johannesburg. Production is in full swing. Techniques for marketing and promotion compete in ingenuity. Capitalism is certainly benefiting, but the demands of bicycle users as regards the organization of work, education and leisure time are such that people now wonder whether the generalized use of bicycles will ultimately open a third political path, one which, situated between liberalism and socialism, is concerned above all with the happiness of individuals. International conferences are being held to study the question. The most recent ones, at the university hub of Aubervilliers, France ('The Bicycle and the End of Ideologies' in 2036, and 'The Bicycle or the Death of God' in 2037), had a worldwide impact. Finally, these handful of successful initiatives have enabled us to realize that the generic

The pedal stroke effect

human (the human being, man or woman, young or old) and his new machine are now as one. The most recent initiative is also the most amazing, and images of it remain forever engraved in memories: ever since the first human pedalled on Mars in front of nine billion Earthlings, something has changed in the history of the planet and in the consciousness of humankind.

Back on Earth

In lingering in utopia, we risk falling from above. And so I will conclude with the above evocation of pedalling in a state of weightlessness. However, we believe now more than ever before that we know weightlessness, or that we know how to recognize it. Images from the world today revive the dream of it when they offer the sight of oversized aeroplanes taking off with several hundred passengers on board; rockets on Cape Canaveral taking off majestically; sparkling megalopolises on our television screens flown over at night by an invisible helicopter; the planet observed by satellites or by fictional characters such as Batman or Spider-Man, whom all the cinematic special effects propel into the four corners of the universe. If these images fascinate us, it is because they illustrate and awaken our desire to escape the heaviness of the everyday. There is no doubt that when they ride a bike people satisfy something of that desire for fluidity, lightness, I was going to say liquidity – that desire which is also expressed in the words they use to talk about the new technology (they 'surf' or 'navigate' the Internet). 'Rivers are paths that move,' Pascal wrote. It is conceivable, inversely, that people have wanted to transform paths into rivers. Moreover, Pascal, it is said, invented the wheelbarrow. Without any other help than the increased strength of one's body, the bicycle in a certain sense enables us to achieve that ideal of easy mobility. The cyclist's dream is to see him or herself on land as the fish is in water or the bird is in the sky, even with the acknowledged constraints of space.

The true advantage of cycling, as opposed to the perhaps overly seductive illusion above, is indeed that it imposes on us a sharper awareness of space, as well as of time. We see this today in Paris where Vélib' bikes pile up at docking stations located at the bottom of hills. The little vans used to replenish empty stations thus function as ski-lifts that enable the lazier riders to indulge in the delights of a heady descent, free-wheeling whenever they want. But even these energy 'freeloaders' are learning in their own way about real space and terrain. If they refuse to ride up the steep rue Saint-Jacques or rue des Martyrs, it is not always out of choice or pure sloth; it is sometimes because of their age or because they are out of shape, and they are aware that they need to work on those weaknesses insofar as they can. They might try again at a later date, after dieting and exercising. The most marvellous quality of the bicycle is that it functions quietly as a friendly biological reminder, just as it requires minimal vigilance by all those who ride.

ANY TENDENCY TOWARDS a passive lifestyle, which for many individuals is strengthened by their connection to various types of media, vanishes as soon as they get on a bike. They assume responsibility for themselves and immediately recognize that responsibility. They become simultaneously aware of the place in which they find themselves, the space in which they can travel in every direction, and of the routes that take them away or bring them home.

When we also take into account the fact that riding a bicycle in general brings back a rider's childhood memories, and they are thereby inspired to reflect on the continuity of their life, we may conclude that the experience of riding a bike is a fundamental existential feat: I pedal, therefore I am.

The current success of the bicycle, notably among young people, is above all revealing. It is like a symptom. Indeed, what escapes us today, in this world of images and media messages, is mainly the principle of reality. We blithely pretend we exist by expressing our opinions far and wide, shaped as they must be by the ambient milieu. We express them to our neighbours when we have them, on the Internet if we know how to navigate it, on TV if we are selected to express ourselves there, or in polls if we are questioned, and even if we aren't, since for the most part polls tell us what we think. The current popularity of bicycles probably comes in part out of that opinion phenomenon. But as soon as we're on the saddle, things change and we find ourselves, we take ourselves in hand. Our personal history takes care of us. The external world is imposed on us concretely in its most physical dimensions. It resists us and forces us to make an effort of will, but at the same time it offers itself to us as a space of intimate freedom and personal initiative, as a *poetic* space, in the full and primary sense of the word.

Children, more so than adults, are naturally philosophical and are constantly wondering. They are not yet *used to*, and the spectacle of inert things surprises them as much as do various forms of biological life. At the same time, children behave as poets, they play, they invent stories. But unlike the adolescent who risks giving in to his fantasies and diurnal dreams, leading him to develop neuroses, as Freud reminds us in his article 'Creative Writers and Day-dreaming', children know how to keep things in perspective and distinguish their play world from reality. Riding a bike in a way gives us back our child's soul and restores both the ability to play and an awareness of the real. It is thus similar to a sort of *refresher* (like a booster vaccination), but also to *continuing education* for learning again about freedom and clarity, and as a result, perhaps, about something that resembles happiness.

Just the fact that riding a bike renders conceivable the dream of a utopian world in which life's pleasures would be everyone's priority, a world that would ensure respect for all, gives us reason to hope. A return to utopia, a return to what is real – they are the same. Get on your bike to improve everyone's life! Cycling is a humanism.